# ST FRANCIS FOR PROTESTANTS
## HENK VAN OS

# ST FRANCIS FOR PROTESTANTS

The exhibition *St Francis of Assisi* in the Catharijneconvent Museum in Utrecht included a superb depiction of the saint receiving the stigmata, painted by Lorenzo Monaco < 1.[1] The story is as follows. In 1224 St Francis went in search of silence in the wild mountain landscape near La Verna, where he utterly immersed himself in the Passion of Christ. Then his Redeemer appeared to him. The crucified Christ was conveyed from a golden sky by a seraph, an angel with six wings. When the angel and crucifix disappeared, St Francis received the wounds of Christ. With his stigmatisation, St Francis's imitation of Christ reached its climax. Two years after this mystical event, in 1226, St Francis died, leaving behind thousands of earthly disciples.

The apostle Paul wrote to the Galatians, 'I bear the wounds (the stigmata) of the Lord Jesus in my body'. What St Paul probably only meant in a figurative sense became literal reality for St Francis. As a result, this mystical experience can be portrayed as an event by artists such as Lorenzo Monaco. This is also how Petrarch chose to understand the stigmatisation. In a letter of 1367 he wrote, 'St Francis felt himself to be one with his Master who was nailed to the Cross, and his pious imagination eventually caused the marks of which he was thinking to appear on his body, where they became tangible reality'.[2] However, there were already intellectuals in the 13th century who, in contrast to Petrarch, did not believe in the stigmatisation of St Francis. Competing orders of mendicant monks such as the Dominicans regularly labelled the stigmatisation as a sort of religious hocus pocus. But then, the head of their order, St Dominic, was not a figure who spoke to the imagination. People who commissioned religious art found little inspiration in a theological dogmatist like him. In contrast, St Francis preached no doctrine, and numerous images of him have been preserved that were produced as early as the 13th century. The first dated depiction of his stigmatisation is in fact dated 1236 < 2 and 3. It is not surprising that such early art works were later claimed as proof that the stigmatisation was genuine.

All those paintings served an ancient function: making the un-imaginable visible. In the midst of the pointless fuss over 'authenticity' that has gone on for centuries, it is best simply to re-read that one sentence of Petrarch, which so superbly describes how the stigmatisation made St Francis into an image of Jesus < 1.

The painting by Lorenzo Monaco occupies a prominent position in the series of early depictions of the stigmatisation. It was painted around 1420, and the artist was the most important Florentine painter at that time. He was a Camaldolese painter monk, who worked primarily for the monastery of Santa Maria degli Angeli. Lorenzo illuminates the mountains of La Verna with the apparition of the crucified Christ borne on wings. The rocks of La Verna heave along with the ecstasy of St Francis. Figure and landscape are over-whelmed by the divine apparition.

The painting is now back in the place where it belongs, in the Rijksmuseum on the wall with many other early Italian paintings. Many of these were once the property of the exuberant collector Otto Lanz. His collection was housed in his colossal house on Museumplein, which later on housed the Boerhaave Clinic < 4 and 5. There, Otto Lanz assembled one of the largest collections of early Italian art that ever existed. The art made the rooms of his villa into the epitome of lavish display < 6. Elsewhere, I have given a detailed description of how much of that art found its way to the Rijksmuseum after the war via the collection of Adolf Hitler. Along with students, I catalogued and exhibited most of the early paintings between the years 1969 and 1988 < 7 and 8.[3]

Our question is: did Lanz buy that painting by Lorenzo Monaco in the 1920s simply because it was a beautiful work of art, or did the depiction of St Francis's mystical experience in the La Verna moun-tains also play a role? Any answer to this question is inevitably hypo-thetical, but all the same I suspect with some certainty that St Francis had a special meaning for Otto Lanz. To prove this, we first have to look at the life history of the collector. Otto Lanz was born in 1865 in Steffisburg in the Bernese Oberland. His father practiced medicine there. Otto was only seven years old when he lost his mother. His grief over her early death accompanied him throughout his life. His governess stated that Otto was originally a religious boy, but later on he drifted away from his faith. According to her, he was a restless young fellow with poor health, which was reason for his father to send him regularly to a farming family living high in the mountains above Eriz. Otto developed a great love for nature there, and grew up amid the drama of the mountains and the ongoing babble of an idyllic country village. In his youth he showed himself to be a passionate collector of natural history objects. From the poems he wrote as a 12-year old, you can gather that he had sublimated his religiosity into an unlimited love for God's creation. *Natur in Fernsicht und Nahsicht* (nature seen from near and far) remained a constant theme of his poetry.

In his youth, Otto attended high school in Bern and studied medicine in Geneva and Basel. In 1879, he became assistant to the world-famous surgeon Theodor Kocher in Bern. During his studies he developed into a textbook example of a *Bildungsbürger*. He knew a great deal about music and enjoyed playing the violin. He knew the great classics of German literature, as is evident from his poems. Additionally, he was a great aficionado of sculpture. Whatever he did, he did with passion. His life unfolded at a constant level of fortissimo, as his biographer wrote. Lanz travelled through Italy with his compatriot Burckhardt's *Cicerone* in his luggage and enjoyed himself enormously. Full of expectations, this tempestuous, flamboyant Swiss came with his wife Anna Willi in 1902 to take a position as professor of surgery at the University of Amsterdam.[4]

After having collected everything from butterflies and plants to uniform buttons and tram tickets, Otto added a number of Italian paintings to his collection in 1896. He had bought them from his violin maker in Bern, and these became the core of his collection. In the 1920s, when he acquired the Lorenzo Monaco, the house on Museumplein was already crammed with early Italian paintings < 9.

Whether he bought the Lorenzo Monaco because of a particular liking for St Francis, or simply because it was another early painting, is impossible to say. Lanz considered himself a Renaissance man, but that does not automatically turn him into a devotee of St Francis.

Fortunately, there is another resource for art-historical research besides text documentation. That resource is seldom referred to as such, but for our field it is very significant. It is called social contact. I can already see a few colleagues out there in the audience knitting their brows, so I will cheerfully repeat: social contact is a significant resource for art-historical research. In our case, this has to do with my friendship with Anna Gertrud, the daughter of Otto Lanz < 10. I made her acquaintance in 1975, when she was already 80 and the widow of the doctor Jo Kijzer, who was the founder of the Dutch Society for Sexual Reform. Mrs Kijzer-Lanz wrote me a letter in connection with the research project 'Early Italian Art in Dutch Collections'. Together with PhD students and with the aid of such figures as Dolf van Asperen de Boer and Ernst van de Wetering, the catalogue *The Florentine Paintings in Holland 1300–1500* had appeared the previous year. It included discussions of numerous paintings from the now dispersed Lanz collection. Mrs Kijzer wrote to me about how grateful she was that her father's paintings were attracting attention for the first time in many years. She added that she possessed rich documentation both for the collection as a whole, and for each individual painting.

I left Groningen immediately for Bachplein 4 in Amsterdam, where she lived with her daughter's family. An incredible surprise awaited me there. Otto's daughter had adored her father. That adoration had taken the form of total service to his activities as a collector. For hours she told tales about her father's paintings, the people who had sold them, the wanderings of the collection during the war, the art-loving visitors to the house on Museumplein like Max Friedländer and Bernard Berenson, the Rijksmuseum and its director Schmidt Degener, and much else as well.

A remarkable document has been preserved to attest to her love and devotion for her father. When Otto Lanz had been professor of surgery for 25 years, the anniversary was lavishly observed. In the Senate Room of the building where find ourselves today, an official portrait of the renowned surgeon was made < 11. There he sits, enthroned amid his wife, children, colleagues and assistants. Everyone is arranged there as they always are in such photographs. They stand where they are expected to. But not his daughter Anna Gertrud. She is not relegated to the background next to her husband, but stands all aglow behind her father's chair, her right hand on his shoulder. Above all, this photograph is a depiction of her devotion and his monumental presence. In the same year (1927) the university invited no less an artist than Jan Toorop to paint a portrait of Otto Lanz < 12.[5] It proved to be a portrait of confrontational frontality. His piercing gaze makes one suspect that this surgeon could perform his own X-rays.

Mrs Kijzer-Lanz enriched our research project enormously with all her information on her father's paintings and even pointed it in a new direction. We all developed a more general interest in the history of the collection and in the provenance of the Italian paintings in particular. I went regularly to Bachplein 4 to ask questions. I have rarely met anyone of her age who exuded such strength, or who spoke with such conviction and persuasive power about the most diverse subjects imaginable. At an early stage, my hostess surprised her family somewhat by asking me to call her by her nickname 'Mimi'. Our conversation and correspondence were no longer only about art, but also about faith. Mimi was a staunch member of the Remonstrant church and I was just an ordinary Dutch Reformed fellow. That difference gave rise to lively discussions. The most beautiful experience I had during our friendship was being her guest for a week in 1979 in the *Hütte*, the vacation house that Otto Lanz had built in the region where he was born, in Eriz, high above Lake Thun < 13. Every year the family sent Mimi up by cable car to this isolated spot to enjoy the summer months there, which she did with gusto. The *Hütte* contained a wood-panelled studio where she liked to pass the time. The room had been inspired by the Albrecht Dürer etching *St Jerome in his Study* 14 >. But the conversations we had while looking out over the Alpine meadow were not about St Jerome, but about St Francis of Assisi! Mimi had decided that it was the aura of St Francis that had connected me to her and her father 15 >. St Francis was her saint. She had made the man from Assisi entirely her own and shaped him to the measure of her feelings for her father and her new friend. She also found that there was a painting that expressed this, and that was Lorenzo Monaco's portrayal of the stig-matisation. There was even a photograph of it on the table. Naturally, I immediately wanted to know whether her father was also such a devotee of St Francis. 'Of course', she replied. Her father's romantic love of nature, especially for the mountain landscape, led him towards the man who so intensely loved the world about him for being God's creation 16 >. This was a more than satisfactory answer to my first question. Yes, Otto Lanz loved St Francis, a saint who retreated to the mountains where he went to encounter his God. Thus, that love of St Francis was genuinely related to his acquisition of the painting by Lorenzo Monaco 17 >.

Besides that photograph of Lorenzo Monaco's painting, two books lay on the table during those days in Eriz, which claimed that St Francis was able to overstep the borders of the Roman Catholic church as an institution, so that for people like us who wanted nothing to do with canonisation, he could become a saint as well. One of these was the book that had also brought me closer to St Francis. In 1958 my mentor Henk Schulte Nordholt presented me with a Phaidon edition of Heinrich Thode's *Francis of Assisi and the Beginnings of Renaissance Art in Italy*. It was first published in 1885 and at the time was viewed primarily as an alternative to Jakob Burckhardt's wildly popular view of the dawn of a new era, in which man discovers both himself and the outside world. To this end, he has to use the help of the heroes of classical antiquity to extricate himself from feudal bonds and free himself from the power of theology and the church. To do this, you need ruthless men who will stop at nothing to achieve it, critical, independent and learned figures.

Heinrich Thode saw such human self-discovery not in terms of liberation from faith, but in the intensification of the individual practice of faith, an intensification that found expression in a new love of nature. He was not interested in having ruthless power figures to act as the principal representatives of a new culture, but pointed to St Francis and his companions, who tried in the midst of poverty and humility to rediscover what faith was, as the great innovators 18 >. Thode had spent days in the upper church of San Francesco in Assisi, which was still quiet in those days, contemplating Giotto's frescoes. Then it occurred to him,

> St Francis of Assisi deepened religious life and gave it warmth …He freed individual feeling from spiritual patronisation and gave it permanent legitimacy …Only now could Christian art be elevated to freedom, because in order to picture the divine it was enough to draw on an ideal from human natural experience.

This is what we spoke of on the Alpine meadow. It brought Mimi into near ecstasy and I was surprised and moved by this completely unexpected confrontation with Thode, whose ideas I had once chosen as the starting point for my own art-historical research. But there was also a second book, and that book was most responsible for the fact that 20th-century devotion to St Francis outside the confines of the church blossomed to such an unprecedented extent. Its author was the Remonstrant Protestant minister Paul Sabatier, and it was called *Vie de saint François d'Assise*, which was published in Paris in 1894. In this work, he presents St Francis with great insight as a free man who undergoes spiritual experiences with great intensity. He is a friend to animals, a poet, and preaches radical poverty. Sabatier means to free him from church and theology, just as Jesus was freed from them by Ernest Renan in his *Vie de Jésus*. Indeed, Renan was the mentor of Sabatier.

In ten years' time, Sabatier's *Life of Saint Francis* had already received its thirtieth printing. When it appeared in 1894, the Vatican immediately placed it on the index of forbidden books. That is not justifiable,

but it is understandable. It was the first historical biography of St Francis, separate from the Lives of the Saints, and in that first true historical study, the seriously historical St Francis is divested of the churchly trappings that Thomas of Celano, St Bonaventure and all the writers of the Lives of the Saints had worked so hard to create. According to Sabatier, St Francis was a radical. He did not belong to one church; his significance is universal. Paul Sabatier made St Francis a topic of salon discussion. His book was even translated into Russian by no less a figure than Tolstoy. Thanks to Paul Sabatier, St Francis became part of the spiritual legacy of every European and of Remonstrant Protestants like Mimi and her father in particular. On the Alpine meadow in the Bernese Oberland, I was further initiated into her spiritual world. It was there that Mimi Lanz read to her friend from Sabatier's *Life of St Francis*.[6]

After Eriz, our contact became somewhat less frequent. Six years later, when she felt the end was near, she informed me that it was time to take our leave of each other. On that occasion, she presented me with a copy of Paul Sabatier's book in the so-called *édition définitive* that appeared in 1931, three years after the author's death. In Eriz we had used an earlier, completely worn-out edition. This new one was intended for me. When I arrived home, I discovered to my utter astonishment that she had filled the whole book with all sorts of pictures and postcards of Assisi, as well as a wealth of newspaper articles on St Francis and Sabatier. Everything was from Remonstrant Protestant circles. As I read, an entirely new St Francis took shape before me, which I want to introduce to you. But first, there is something about two of those postcards.

The postcards originated from two notable followers of Lanz. It seems that the professor sent these two gentlemen to Assisi in connection with the principle of 'whoever wants to know St Francis must go to Assisi'. One postcard is dated 23 March 1925 and was written by Jan van Heek. From what he writes, we see that Otto Lanz also made purchases for his friends' collections, as he refers to a St Francis by the 15th-century painter Vittorio Crivelli, which Lanz bought for him in Paris. This painting was presumably destroyed during the 1939 fire of Huis Bergh in 's Heerenbergh, but there are still two paintings by the same Vittorio Crivelli of the Franciscan saints Anthony of Padua and Bernardine of Siena 19 >. It is likely that these made up part of the same Franciscan altarpiece as the painting of St Francis.[7] Moreover, in 1926 Jan van Heek bought a lovely painting of St Francis, most certainly with Otto Lanz as an intermediary, which has been preserved. It shows the saint appearing in Arles to St Anthony and his brothers, painted by the Sienese painter Taddeo di Bartolo 20 >.[8]

The second postcard from 1925 came from Otto Lanz's friend, the collector Edwin von Rath, for whom Lanz also purchased a number of works. Since 1941, Rath's collection of approximately 50 Italian paintings has been part of the collections of the Rijksmuseum.[9] The text on both cards makes it clear that the men's visit to Assisi amounted to the completion of an assignment from the professor. Among all the articles that I discovered carefully folded up in Sabatier's book were five reflections on St Francis by the minister who was to become a star of the Remonstrant Protestant radio network VPRO, J.C.A. Fetter of Rotterdam. They were published in the Remonstrant religious weekly magazine *De Stroom (The Current)* and came from 1926, the year in which the 700th anniversary of the death of St Francis was commemorated throughout Europe and America. In those five extensive articles from the 'Personalities' column, Dr Fetter presents his St Francis, who also became the St Francis that Mimi and her father knew. He shows that the church and the monasteries had given themselves up to greed at the time that St Francis preached against the sinfulness of Christian institutions. Dr Fetter paints a vivid picture of his hero's life. In the fourth article he emphasises the necessity of teaching a sense of duty in our economic dealings. For him, the era of *Naturalwirtschaft* is gone forever. Couldn't we say to Francis, 'Dear St Francis, we don't long for poverty, but we do want simplicity and a dignified existence for all people. Our society strives for this despite all forces that oppose it.' That word 'simplicity' became a shibboleth in those years: it was the personification of ideal living for well-to-do and well-meaning citizens. It was the foundation for personal and societal ethics, and for aesthetics as well. St Francis is the incarnation of these Remonstrant Protestant virtues.

In the fifth article, Dr Fetter directly addresses the 'group of Remonstrant Christians'.

> We Remonstrant Christians are called to orientate ourselves towards the most spiritual words and stories that we find in the New Testament and in the Franciscan legends ... The symbolic Christ and St Francis figures are not <u>people</u> that we are called on to imitate, for in order to be ourselves and live in our own era, we must imitate no one. Instead, they are fundamental principles that must live <u>within us</u> as much as possible and <u>from which</u> we must live to the best of our ability.

The minister has made his point clearly. There is both a historical St Francis and a symbolic St Francis, and we can cleanse that symbolic St Francis of everything that does not suit us in the historical figure and thus 'elevate him above ecclesiastical boundaries'. These last words are by Prof. L. J. van Holk, who was later sometimes referred to as 'the Remonstrant Pope'. On behalf of all Remonstrant Christians, he expresses thanks to Paul Sabatier for having discovered St Francis for him.[10] In contrast to the Remonstrant Protestants, it is striking that Dutch Reformed Protestants, while fellow Christians, recognise neither a symbolic Christ nor a symbolic St Francis, as I ascertained from the rich documentation of Nico ter Linden and Jan Greven. Apparently they were too scripture- and history-orientated for that.

However, the notion of a 'symbolic figure' is crucial to an accurate understanding of the 20th-century St Francis, a saint who is no longer the sole property of the church of the veneration of the saints.

Remarkably diverse individuals and groups of people have distilled their own symbolic figures from the story of St Francis, producing an astounding wealth of representations. Of course the saintly-ecological aspect was most popular both within and outside the church, but St Francis was also declared patron saint of Italy by Pope Pius XI in the ominous year of 1938. In South America St Francis played a major role as a source of inspiration in liberation theology. In the eyes of revolutionaries there, he became an example of solidarity with the poor. Radicals of every stripe revere St Francis for his inspiring qualities. Everyone has his own St Francis. I would like to illustrate this in audible and visible form, first with two texts, then with six illustrations.

The first text is by the great playwright Oscar Wilde 21 >. In 1895 he was convicted of sodomy. In prison he wrote the letter that was to become famous, his *De Profundis*. In it he professes his love for Jesus and St Francis. I quote,

> It is the imaginative quality of Christ's own nature that makes him this palpitating centre of romance... He has all the colour of life: mystery, strangeness, pathos, suggestion, ecstasy, love... The unfortunate thing is that there have been none since. I make an exception, St Francis of Assisi...with the soul of a poet and the body of a beggar he found the way to perfection not difficult. He understood Christ so he became like him.

Everyone knows St Francis. In any case, that was the assumption made by Margaret Thatcher on 4 May 1979 when she took charge of 10 Downing Street as the new Prime Minister of the United Kingdom 22 >. I quote,

> And I would just like to remember some words of St Francis of Assisi which I think are really just particularly apt at the moment. 'Where there is discord, may we bring harmony. Where there is error, may we bring truth. Where there is doubt, may we bring faith. And where there is despair, may we bring hope.'

Actually, these are not the words of St Francis, but the words with which she hopes to impose his authority. It is the St Francis of Margaret Thatcher.[11]

In the field of visual art as well, every artist has his own St Francis.

1. Around 1900, St Francis was a favourite subject in symbolist art, as can be seen from this evocative portrayal of St Francis and poverty, a painting from around 1900 by Giuseppe Mentessi **23 >**.

2. What can happen with a St Francis shorn of ecclesiastical purposes is shown by a crazy 1935 painting by Sir Stanley Spencer in the Tate Gallery **24 >**. It prominently depicts St Francis as a merrily gesticulating, bearded, fat man. His habit is not brown, but green, because the model was the painter's father who was wearing his green housecoat. The poultry we see surrounding this fat Francis came from Cookham, the village in Berkshire where Spencer was born. This bizarre painting was rejected by the Royal Academy, but what does one rejection matter in the face of this delightful exception to the long line of depictions of St Eco-Francis?

3. The story of St Francis preaching to the birds has inspired the imagination of artists to take flight time and time again. My colleagues Eddy de Jong and Jan Piet Filedt Kok drew my attention to drawings by Peter Vos, who created a gripping image of the birds who here for once do not listen, but overwhelm St Francis by preaching back *en masse!* **25 >**[12]

4. Even the stigmatisation, a story that is smoothed over by non-ecclesiastical venerators of St Francis because of its supernatural quality, can provide an impulse for new and highly original secular representations. A splendid example of this is in the collections of the Groninger Museum. It is a cosmic vision on a large scale, drawn in charcoal by Enzo Cucchi in 1981. In this work he fuses the sky and the hills with hands bearing the stigmata **26 >**.

5. This year I received a New Year's card from Co Westerik titled *The Wounded Foot*. Maybe it is an aberration caused by my line of work, but the only way I could perceive it was as one of the stigmata with a sacred aura. In any case, it is a religious variant of the finger that is cut on a blade of grass **27 >**.

6.   The last picture in this series is an obvious homage to the 1962 painting *Blam* by Roy Liechtenstein. It is a photo collage van Benoît Hermans. The artist shows Murillo's St Francis floating into the picture with the hand of Christ on his shoulder. The saint is trying to hold on to an exploding aeroplane that is about to crash upside down. Hermans titles his hard-hitting image *Imitatio Christi*. It will be clear to you here that free association is permitted. Not only does everyone have his own St Francis- it can be worthwhile to have some good fun with the saint from Assisi 28 >.[13]

These six examples should suffice to make you aware of the impressive variety of representations of St Francis and of images related to him. I also intended them as a plea for arranging art of our time in these iconographical categories now and then, if for no other reason that it produces one surprise after the other. To date, absolutely no work has been done on St Francis iconography of the 20th century.[14] There is one observation I would like to share with you. Amid all that diversity, there is one constant factor. There is one St Francis that has been seen all over the world for a century, and it looks like the bust surrounded by flowers in front of this lectern 29 >. It is the very image of the 'symbolic' St Francis as described by the Remonstrant minister Fetter. It is the countenance of a quiet, introverted, handsome young man, gentle, loving, tender, turned towards inner life. The Remonstrant ministers' qualifications of St Francis are all applicable to this fragile man of glazed terra cotta. I found it in an unusual way. My wife and I were having lunch with friends. He was telling us about his family, which was full of Remonstrant ministers. 'Are you called Frans because of St Francis?' I asked. 'Absolutely,' was the answer. 'Just wait a minute.' And Frans carried this St Francis from downstairs. It is the perfect image of St Francis for Remonstrants. This is St Francis as Mimi Lanz pictured him.

Does this idealised symbolic figure have any relationship to the descriptions of the real St Francis, with the historical figure? The answer is no. Contemporaries described him as an unsightly man with a black, unkempt beard. They speak of the intensity of his conversation and of how charismatic his pronouncements were, whether they were fire-and-brimstone sermons or glorifications of God's creation. He was a theatrical man marked by a life of rugged asceticism, a cave dweller, who made both city and countryside tremble at times with his message of radical poverty. When everything became too much for him, he retreated again to a life of fasting and prayer in the mountains. If you are looking for the historical person St Francis while in Assisi, you must not look at the art and the beautiful buildings. All that beauty was completely at odds with his ideal of poverty. If you want the historical St Francis, then you must go to the *Eremo dei Carceri* **30** >. St Francis lived there. Someone might be wondering now, why should you then pay attention to such a sickly sweet, symbolic figure like this one? Because it so well embodies the values and ideals that people in our time cherish, and that they project onto figures from the past. And those values and ideals are constantly dashed to bits against the harsh reality of life, and of history as well.

1   V.M. Schmidt, in Exhibition catalogue, *Lorenzo Monaco*, ed. A. Tartuferi/D. Parenti, Florence 2006, No. 35, p. 204–208, with painstaking references to older literature.

2   On Petrarch's description of the stigmatisation: M. Bishop, *St Francis of Assisi*, Boston, 1974. Dutch translation, Schoten, 1976, p. 163. On the stigmatisation as an image of Jesus: H. Belting. Francis: The Body as Image, in *Image and Body in the Middle Ages*. K. Marek, R. Preisinger, M. Rimmele, K. Kärcher (Eds.), Paderborn 2006, p. 21–37.

3   H.W. van Os. Otto Lanz and the collection of early Italian art in the Netherlands, *Bulletin of the Rijksmuseum* 26 (1978), p. 147–174. For an overview of the publications for the project *Early Italian Paintings in the Netherlands*, idem, in *The Early Sienese Paintings in Holland*, ed. H.W. van Os, J.R.J. van Asperen de Boer, C.E. de Jong-Janssen, C. Wiethoff. Florence, 1989, p. 9–11.

4   Most of the information on Otto Lanz is taken from an unpublished biography by Adolf Schaer-Ris, *Otto Lanz: Life and Work of a Surgeon, Poet, Politician and Art Collector, 1865–1932*, Sigriswil, 1939 (completed and revised, 1944). Thanks to the admirable detective work of Freek Heybroek, the manuscript was preserved. Due to his generosity, I was the first person to make use of this valuable text for this publication. In 2008 Fee van 't Veen devoted much attention to Otto Lanz in *Palazzo: On Early Italian Art Collected in the Netherlands Between 1900 and 1940*, a publication of the Bonnefantenmuseum in Maastricht. A copy of her highly readable doctoral dissertation *Lanz's Taste* is contained in the library of the Rijksmuseum.

5   G. van Wezel, Exhibition catalogue, *Jan Toorop, Zang der Getijden (Song of Time)*, Gemeentemuseum, Den Haag, No. 427, p. 260.

6   On the meaning of Paul Sabatier's *Life of Saint Francis*: A. Vauchez, *Francis of Assisi: The Life and Afterlife of a Medieval Saint*. New Haven/London 2012, p. 234–238.

7   J.H. van Heek, Huis Bergh: Castle and Collection, ed. R.R.A. van Gruting, Nijmegen, 1987, p. 157, Ill. p. 154, 155. I. Dragt, in *The Early Venetian Paintings in Holland*, ed. H.W. van Os, J.R.J. van Asperen de Boer, C.E. de Jong-Jansen, C. Wiethoff. Maarssen, 1978, p. 72–77. Both panels originate from an altarpiece in San Francesco, Fermo.

8   M. Brüggen Israëls. St Francis in Early Italian Art, in Exhibition catalogue, *St Francis of Assisi*, Museum Catharijneconvent, Utrecht, 2016, p. 85–87, 198. The panel originates from the main altarpiece of San Francesco, Perugia.

9   F. van 't Veen, op. cit. note 4, p. 67–69, 85.

10  The articles by J.C.A. Fetter are found in the issues of *The Current* of 18 and 25 September and 2,9 and 16 October 1926. L. J. van Holk acknowledged his affection for St Francis and his dependence on Sabatier in a radio lecture for the VPRO on 10 October 1926, as well as an article in *De Smidse (The Forge)* on the occasion of the Dutch translation of Sabatier's book.

11  www.margaretthatcher.org/document/104078.

12  J.P. Filedt Kok, E de Jongh. *Peter Vos and Charles Donker*, Utrecht 2010, p. 18.

13  F. van der Schoor, in *From Trajan to Tajiri: Collection Museum Het Valkhof Nijmegen*, Nijmegen 2009, p. 86.

14  Referring to: Representative aspects of art works, in *The Art of the 20th Century*. E. de Jongh, op. cit. note 12, p. 22–23.

The publication of this book was made possible
in part by a grant from the University of Amsterdam
on the occasion of the valedictory address of
Henk van Os.

Translator: David Barick
Design: Irma Boom Office
Paper: Igepa Muskat Grey 140 gsm

Amsterdam University Press English-language titles
are distributed in the US and Canada by the
University of Chicago Press.

ISBN        978 94 6298 502 5
e-ISBN      978 90 4853 596 5
NUR         640

Former home of the Lanz family
(photo: author's collection)

< 6 Glimpse into the house of the
Lanz family
(photo: author's collection)

< 7 Arrangement of early Italian paintings
in the renovated Rijksmuseum
(photo: Rijksmuseum)

< **8** see < **1**

< **9** A small chamber in the house of the Lanz family
(photo: author's collection)

< **11** 25th anniversary professorship of Otto Lanz
(photo: author's collection)

< **10** Anna Gertrud Kijzer-Lanz
(photo: Lanz family collection)